Look What You Can Make With

Egg Cartons

Edited by Betsy Ochester
Photographs by Hank Schneider

Boyds Mills Press

Craft Coordinator:

Betsy Ochester

Contributors:

Patricia Barley
Katherine Bartow
Anne Bell
Frances M. Callahan
Marie E. Cecchini
Mary Colacurcio
Sandra Csippan
Kathy Everett

Vicki Felix
Marguerite Harrington
Carmen Horn
Helen Jeffries
Tama Kain
Garnett Kooker
Lee Lindeman
Betsy Ochester

James W. Perrin, Jr.
Sylvia W. Sproat
Matthew Stockton
Debora Sullivan
Sharon Dunn Umnik
Francis Wales
D. A. Woodliff

Copyright © 2000 by Boyds Mills Press
All rights reserved

Published by Bell Books
Boyds Mills Press, Inc.
A Highlights Company
815 Church Street
Honesdale, Pennsylvania 18431
Printed in China

U.S. Cataloging-in-Publication Data
    (Library of Congress Standards)

Look what you can make with egg cartons : over 90 pictured crafts and dozens of other ideas /
edited by Betsy Ochester ; photographs by Hank Schneider. --1st ed.
[48] p. : col. ill. ; cm.
Summary: Toys, games, and other ideas all from egg cartons.
ISBN: 1-56397-906-3
1. Box craft. 2. Handicraft. I. Ochester, Betsy. II. Schneider, Hank, ill. III. Title.
745.54 --21 2000   AC CIP
00-100007

First edition, 2000
Books in this series originally designed by Lorianne Siomades
The text of this book is set in 10pt Avant Garde Demi, titles 43pt Gill Sans Extra Bold

10 9 8 7 6 5 4 3 2 1

Getting Started

This book is filled with fun, easy-to-make crafts, and each one begins with an egg carton. You'll find a wide variety of things to make, including toys, games, and gifts.

Directions

Before you start each craft, read the directions and look closely at the photograph, but remember—it's up to you to make the craft your own. If we decorate a craft with markers, but you want to use glitter paint and stickers, go for it. Feel free to stray from our directions and invent new crafts.

Work Area

It's a good idea to keep your work area covered. Old newspapers, brown paper (from grocery bags), or old sheets work well. Also, protect your clothes by wearing a smock. A big, old shirt does the job and gives you room to move. Finally, remember to clean up when you've finished.

Materials

You'll need a lot of egg cartons, so start saving now. Ask friends and relatives to help. Keep your craft-making supplies together, and before making each craft, check the "You Will Need" list to make sure you have everything. In this list, we'll often specify whether we used plastic-foam or cardboard egg cartons. For some crafts, however, either type will work. Also, since you'll need scissors and glue, tape, or a stapler for almost every craft, we don't list these supplies.

Other Stuff

When we show several similar crafts, we'll often list numbered directions that apply to all of the crafts, then specific directions for each craft.

Important egg-carton terms: In our directions, we refer to the parts of the carton that hold the eggs as "cups" or "egg cups." The bottom of the cup is the part on which the egg sits. A "peak" refers to the cone shape that is in between the cups.

Here's a painting tip: Poster paint won't stick to plastic-foam egg cartons (though it works great for cardboard cartons). Try mixing liquid soap with the paint. It works for us.

That's about all. So, find a bunch of egg cartons, select a craft that you like, and have some fun. Before you know it, you'll be showing everyone what you made with egg cartons.

Critter Keepers

Need a place to store small treasures? These adorable animals can help!

You Will Need:

- felt
- egg cartons
- markers
- toothpicks
- plastic wiggle eyes
- foam paper
- plastic-foam balls
- construction paper
- chenille sticks

To Make the Basic Container

1 Cut a piece of felt big enough to cover the lid of an egg carton. It should be at least 7 inches by 15 inches in size. Glue the felt to the lid, tucking in the edges as you would gift wrap and gluing them securely. Let the glue dry.

2 Follow the directions for the animal you want to make.

To Make the Hedgehog

For the quills, use markers to color wooden toothpicks. Dip the end of each quill into glue, then poke it into the top of the lid. Glue on wiggle eyes, and a nose and mouth cut from foam paper.

To Make the Frog

For the eyes, glue two plastic-foam balls to the top of the carton and glue a black paper circle to each. Cut out a tongue shape from red foam paper and add detail with marker. Glue the tongue in place on the inside of the lid.

Make the creatures shown here, or create your own—just about any animal can be a critter keeper.

To Make the Lobster

To make the eyes, poke a piece of white chenille stick into each of two plastic-foam balls. Use a toothpick to poke two holes in the top of the egg carton. Insert the chenille sticks into the holes with a little glue. Cut claws from foam paper, and glue them to the inside of the lid. Glue on wiggle eyes and a foam-paper mouth.

To Make the Blue Whale

Fold a piece of blue felt in half. Cut a tail shape from the felt, using the fold as the top of the tail. Place two chenille sticks between the felt pieces, leaving about 1 inch of each stick poking out from the bottom of the tail. Glue the pieces of felt together. When the glue is dry, bend into a curved shape. Poke the two ends of the chenille sticks into the back of the carton, bend them, and add glue to secure. Glue on wiggle eyes and features cut from foam paper.

More Ideas

Use a critter keeper as a desk organizer to hold paper clips, erasers, and rubber bands. Or place one on a bathroom counter to store cotton balls and swabs.

For Halloween, make a monster critter keeper. Fill it with candy and give it to a friend for an extra-special treat.

Great-Shape Necklace

Make your own fashion statement with this unique necklace.

You Will Need:

- plastic-foam egg carton
- markers
- drinking straws
- string or yarn
- needle

1 Cut shapes from the lid of the egg carton and color them with markers. Cut out small pieces of the drinking straws. Cut a piece of string or yarn long enough to fit over your head. Thread one end of the string onto the needle.

2 String a shape and then a section of straw onto the string, leaving an inch of string at the bottom. Continue stringing the shapes and straws until you almost have reached the end of the string. Tie the two ends of the string together.

More Ideas

Necklaces are just the beginning of the egg-carton jewelry you can make. String together bracelets for your wrists and ankles. Create a ring by poking a few shapes onto a piece of chenille stick, and wrapping it around your finger. Or design a decorative belt by stringing shapes onto a strong piece of twine.

Ladybug Pin

This colorful friend will brighten your shirt, jacket, or backpack.

You Will Need:

- egg carton
- markers or paint
- cotton balls
- poster board
- black yarn
- safety pin

1 Cut one cup from the egg carton. Trim it into a ladybug shape. Color the cup with a red marker or paint. Draw on a black head, spots, and a line to separate the wings.

2 Glue cotton balls to the inside of the cup. Attach a piece of poster board with glue to the bottom of the cup and cotton balls. Let the glue dry, then trim around the edges of the poster board with scissors. Glue legs, made from short pieces of yarn, to the poster board. Tape or glue a safety pin to the bottom of the ladybug.

More Ideas

Make matching ladybug pins. Give one to a friend, and keep one for yourself.

Instead of a safety pin, glue a piece of magnetic strip to the ladybug to make a refrigerator magnet.

Fun Fliers

Recycle your family's egg cartons into your own fleet of planes. Then zoom into the wild blue yonder!

You Will Need:

- plastic-foam egg cartons
- straight pins
- paint
- markers
- stickers

To Make the Planes

1 On the lid of a plastic-foam egg carton, draw the body, wings, and tail of the airplane you want to make. (Look at the pictures to determine the shapes of these pieces.) Cut out the shapes.

2 Carefully cut slits into the plane's body for the wings and the tail. Insert the wings and the tailpiece into the slits.

3 Follow the instructions for the plane you want to make.

To Make the Biplane

Make a short slit beneath the bottom wing. Insert a small rectangle cut from the lid and bend it to form a stand for the plane. Cut a propeller from the lid and attach it to the front of the plane with a straight pin. Color the plane with markers or paint.

To Make the Jet

For engines, cut small oval pieces from the egg carton and glue them under the wings. Decorate the plane with paint or markers.

To Make the Blue Plane

Attach a propeller as described for the biplane. Cut small circles from the egg carton lid for wheels, and glue them in place. Decorate the plane with paint, markers, and stickers.

More Ideas

Make a runway for your planes by cutting strips from the lid of an egg carton and gluing them together. Use a small box to create a hangar to park your planes when they're on the ground.

Design Your Own Doll Furniture

This doll furniture is beautiful and easy to make, too.

You Will Need:

- cardboard egg cartons
- paint
- clear nail polish (optional)
- ruler

1 Cut the lids from two egg cartons. Follow the directions for the piece of furniture you want to make.

2 Paint the pieces as you wish. We chose flowers and dots as decorations. You might decide to make a striped couch or polka-dotted chairs. If you want to give your furniture a glazed finish, add a coat of clear nail polish.

To Make the Kitchen Table

Cut a flat circle from the lid. Make legs by cutting three strips from the top of the lid that each extend about ¾ of an inch into the side of the lid. Overlap these three legs, and glue the ¾-inch ends to the bottom of the table.

To Make the Straight Chairs

Cut a piece from the side and bottom of the lid. For legs, cut two strips from the side of the lid that each extend about ¾ of an inch into the top of the lid. Overlap these two strips, and glue the ¾-inch ends to the bottom of the chair. Trim the legs so the chair stands evenly.

You'll want to create enough to fill an entire dollhouse!

To Make the Couch

Cut off the end of a lid for the seat. For the legs, cut off an inch-wide lid section next to your previous cut. Glue the legs to the bottom of the seat.

To Make the Armchairs

For the seat, cut off a corner of a lid. Trim it into an armchair shape. Add legs as for the straight chair.

To Make the Coffee Table

Cut a strip from the middle of the lid, including the sides. Cut legs into the sides of the strip.

To Make the Couch Pillow

Glue the ends of two egg-carton cups together to form a pillow shape.

More Ideas

Make an egg-carton tea set for your larger dolls. Cut out individual egg cups for teacups. Add chenille-stick handles. A square of four egg cups can be a caddy to carry your tea cups. Cut round pieces from the lid for saucers. Add a creamer and a sugar bowl made from egg cups. Decorate with paint and markers. Invite all your dolls and stuffed animals for tea!

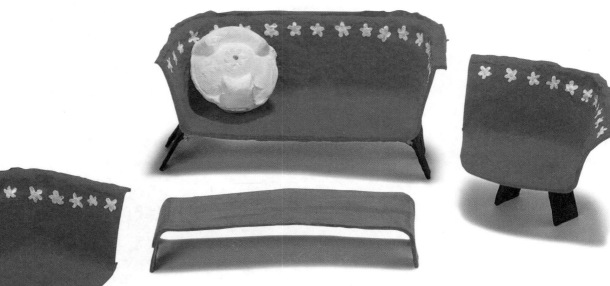

Colossal Castle

Be the king or queen—and the architect—of your own castle. Ask friends and family to start saving egg cartons now—this kingdom calls for a royal number of cartons.

You Will Need:

- seventeen cardboard egg cartons
- large pieces of construction paper
- paint
- large piece of cardboard
- poster board
- craft sticks
- one plastic-foam egg carton
- toothpicks
- markers

2 To make each wall, cut a cardboard egg-carton bottom in half. Glue the two halves together by overlapping three cups. Make "feet" for each wall to stand on by cutting slits at the bottom of two cups and inserting the bottom edge of the wall into the slits. Paint each wall.

3 Cover the large piece of cardboard with green poster board. Glue the towers and walls in place onto the poster board.

4 Cut a gate from poster board and glue the sides to the two front towers. Make a bridge by cutting off two-thirds of a lid, and gluing four cups to it for supports. Paint craft sticks and glue them to the top of the bridge. Glue the bridge in front of the castle.

5 Glue on a moat cut from blue poster board. Make a "moat monster" from scraps cut from a plastic-foam egg carton (our monster's head is half of the lid's raised peak). Add flags made from paper and toothpicks. Draw on windows with a marker.

More Ideas

Make trees for your castle by gluing a stack of egg-carton cups on top of one another, and painting them green. Make finger-puppet dolls to inhabit your kingdom. (To make a basic doll shape, see pages 24-25.) Color one silver for a knight, and give one an aluminum foil crown for a king or queen.

1 To make each of the towers, cut four lids from cardboard cartons. Cut off the short ends from two of the lids. Fit the four lids together, with the two trimmed lids inside the other two, to form a rectangle. Staple or glue the lids together. Cover each tower with construction paper. Cut out four four-cup sections from the cartons, paint them, and glue one on top of each tower.

Egg-Carton Greetings

Instead of buying cards from a store, create your own original works of art.

You Will Need:

- egg carton
- paper
- ink pads

1 Cut off parts of the egg carton that have unusual shapes or patterns to use as stamps.

2 Cut a piece of paper to the size you'd like and fold it in half.

3 Press your egg carton parts onto ink pads. Then press them on the front of the card to create a design. Let your creativity shine! You can make abstract designs or realistic drawings. Write a message inside the card.

More Ideas

Use your egg carton pieces to design wrapping paper. Spread out a large sheet of paper, and stamp away. To make special stationery, stamp shapes around the edges of writing paper.

Pumpkin-Patch Pals

This spirited trio will add spice to your Halloween decorating.

You Will Need:

- cardboard egg carton
- paint
- construction paper

1 Cut six cups from the egg carton. Glue them together in pairs to make three pumpkins. Paint them orange.

2 Cut a section of three peaks from the egg carton for the base. Trim two peaks different heights. Paint the base black.

3 Glue the pumpkins to the base. Attach cut-paper features to the pumpkins. Place your jack-o'-lanterns on a windowsill or table.

More Ideas

Make lots of egg-carton jack-o'-lanterns, without the base, and hand them out with candy to trick-or-treaters.

Halloween Hangers

These spooky mobiles will bring fleets of ghastly ghosts, batty bats, and "boo-tiful" black cats to your Halloween party. They'll also bring lots of smiles to your guests.

You Will Need:

- plastic-foam egg cartons
- hole punch
- yarn
- cardboard egg carton
- paint
- construction paper
- beads
- markers
- thread
- tree branch

To Make the Ghost Mobile

To make the top, cut the bottom section of a white plastic-foam egg carton in half. Poke a hole in each of the four corner cups. Thread a piece of yarn through each hole and knot the yarn. Join the four pieces of yarn in one knot for a hanger. With a hole punch, make holes to hang the ghosts.

For each ghost, cut five cups from a white plastic-foam egg carton. Poke a hole in the bottom of each cup. Tie a knot at the end of a piece of yarn, and thread a bead onto the yarn. Then thread on one egg cup, then two beads, then another egg cup. Continue in this way until you have put on five cups. Then tie a knot at the top of the ghost's head, and tie the end of the yarn to the top section. Draw on faces with a marker.

To Make the Black Cat Mobile

For the top, cut the lid of a plastic-foam egg carton in half, then cut out a square from the middle of that half. Use the hole punch to make holes in each corner and one hole for each cat. Tie a piece of yarn to each corner hole, and join these four pieces in a knot for a hanger.

For each cat, cut one cup from a cardboard egg carton and trim it into the shape of a cat's head, leaving on pointy ears. Paint the heads black. Glue on paper whiskers and eyes. Poke a hole in the top of each cat's head, and tie a piece of yarn to it. Cover the back of each head with a circle of black paper. Tie each cat to a hole in the top section.

To Make the Bat Mobile

For each bat, cut two cups from a plastic-foam egg carton. Make wings and ears from black paper, and glue them between the cups. Add hole-punch eyes and a mouth. Glue or tape a piece of thread to each bat and tie them to a fallen tree branch. Tie three pieces of yarn to the branch, and gather the pieces in a knot for a hanger.

More Ideas

Egg cartons can be turned into all kinds of mobiles—not just Halloween ones. Make an Easter-egg mobile by gluing pairs of egg-carton cups together to make egg shapes. Paint the "eggs" bright colors and tie them to a hanger. Pairs of cups can also be decorated to make a solar-system mobile, an insect mobile, and a baseball mobile. Can you come up with other ideas?

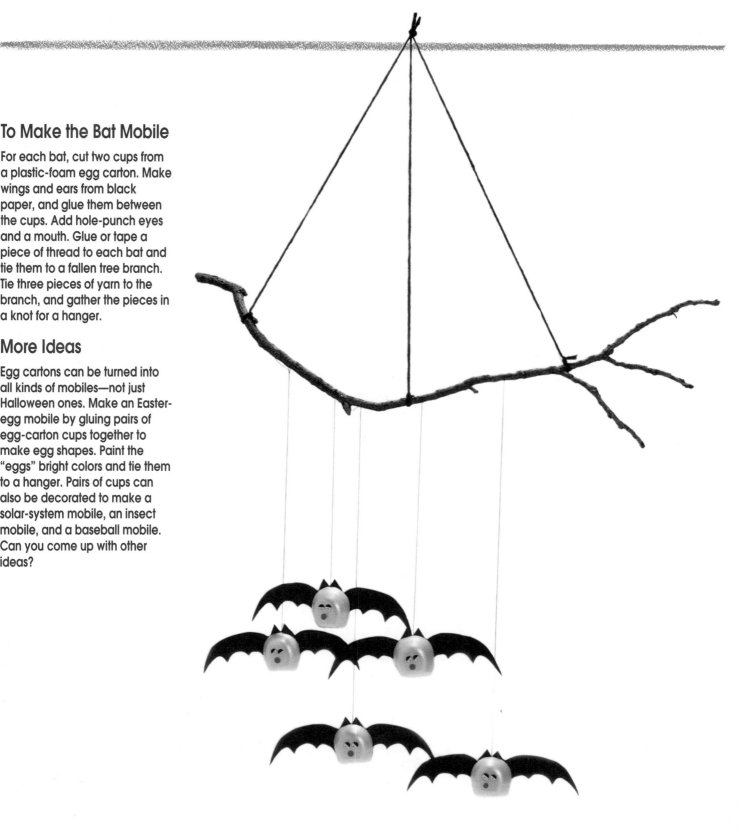

Windowsill Menorah

This Hanukkah decoration can be used year after year.

1 Cut out two rows of egg-carton cups: one row of six and one of three. Stuff each cup with a piece of crumpled tissue paper.

2 Measure and cut a 3-inch-by-19-inch rectangle from the cardboard. Glue the cups, with the stuffed side down, in one straight row, to the cardboard. When the glue has dried, cover the entire menorah with aluminum foil. Crunch the foil around each cup and tape it to the bottom of the cardboard.

3 Color nine craft sticks with a marker. Cut out nine "flames" from construction paper. Glue a flame to the top of each stick. Cut a small slit at the top of each egg cup. Using a little glue, slide the craft sticks into the slits, placing the middle stick slightly higher than the rest.

More Ideas

Instead of gluing the flames to the sticks, use a loop of tape and "light" a new candle for each night of Hanukkah.

Egg-Carton Carolers

Add a festive note to any holiday gathering with this charming chorus.

1 Glue gift wrap to the top of the egg carton, tucking the edges inside the carton. Turn the carton over.

2 With a hole punch, make eyes and mouths from construction paper. Glue them to the twelve egg sections. Cut bow ties from construction paper, and glue them in place. Make hair by gluing strands of yarn to the top of each head. Draw on noses.

3 Write the name of your favorite Christmas carol on a strip of paper. Add musical notes, and glue the paper to the front of the carton.

More Ideas

Place a small cassette player behind the carolers, and play a tape of Christmas music.

Make choruses for other occasions, such as a birthday or anniversary.

Dump Truck

Haul loads around your bedroom with this working dump truck.

You Will Need:

- plastic-foam egg cartons
- construction paper
- ruler
- drinking straw
- chenille stick
- markers

3 For the bed of the truck, cut off a little less than half of a lid. Cut a 3¾-inch-long piece from a drinking straw. Tape this to the bottom of the bed, about ¾ of an inch from the bed's back end. Place the bed on the body, fitting the straw into the notches you made in step 1. Insert a chenille stick through the straw. Twist the stick's ends together under the bumpers to fasten the bed of the truck to the body. This will allow your truck to "dump."

4 To make the tires, cut the tips from four egg-carton cups and glue them to the wheels. Decorate the truck with markers and paper. We made a paper license plate and glued it over the chenille stick.

More Ideas

Create train cars from the lids and bottoms of egg cartons. Connect the cars with short pieces of chenille sticks. Make a track with strips cut from carton lids.

1 For the bottom of the truck, cut a six-cup section from an egg carton, leaving on a small part of the seventh and eighth cups for back bumpers. Cut off the bottoms of the two middle cups; the other four cups will be the truck's wheels. Turn the piece over so that the four "wheels" are facing down. At the top of the body, cut a notch between each of the rear wheels and their "bumper." The two notches should be directly across from each other. Cut a piece of paper to fit over the six-cup section and glue it on top of the body, making sure it doesn't cover the notches.

2 For the truck's cab, cut a two-cup section from the end of an egg carton. Glue it in place on the body.

Cruising Cartons

You're the captain! Build one of these boats, or design your own floatable fleet.

You Will Need:

- plastic-foam egg cartons
- ruler
- craft sticks
- craft spoons
- permanent markers
- paint
- toothpick

To Make the Rowboat

Remove the lid from an egg carton and cut it in half. Turn this half-lid section over so the flat part is facing down. This will be your boat. With scissors, make a 3-inch-long slit on each side of the boat at the spot where the side meets the floor. Then make cuts on the boat floor from the middle of the front of the boat to the far end of each slit. This will leave a triangle shape on the boat's floor. Bend the two sides in to meet the point of the triangle, and tape securely in place.

To add a seat, cut two small slits on opposite sides of the boat. Insert a craft stick. Make oars by cutting slits on opposite sides of the boat and inserting craft spoons. Color your boat with permanent markers.

To Make the Barge

Remove the lid from an egg carton and turn it upside down to form the bottom of the boat. Cut a four-cup section from the carton and glue it onto the lid. Paint craft sticks and glue them onto the rest of the lid. Add life preservers cut from the bottoms of egg cups. Glue on a smokestack made from the raised peak in a carton's lid. Color the boat with permanent markers.

Then take your vessels sailing in a pond, stream, sink, or bathtub.

To Make the Cruise Ship

To make the bottom level of the ship, turn an egg carton over so the cup section is facing up. To form the second level, cut the lid from another carton in half and turn it upside down. Cut flat pieces from another lid and glue them across the top and back of the half-lid to enclose it. Glue the second level to the bottom level.

Next, cut a section of four cups from the end of a carton and glue that on top of the second level. Glue on a smokestack made from the raised peak in a carton's lid. Make a flag by cutting a triangle from a carton and taping it to a toothpick. Color the ship with permanent markers.

More Ideas

Take bath toys for rides on the barge and rowboat. Store soap in the bottom of the cruise ship.

Beautiful Bouquet

Long after ordinary flowers would wilt, these bright blossoms will keep their beauty. Display them as a cheery centerpiece for family meals.

You Will Need:

- cardboard egg cartons
- plastic-foam egg cartons
- chenille sticks
- paint
- old water or soda bottle
- small pebbles
- gift wrap

To Make the Daffodils

For the petal section, cut one cup from a cardboard egg carton and trim the edges. For the flower's center, use a peak cut from the carton.

To Make the Tulips

Cut one cardboard egg cup for the petal section. Bend a short piece of black chenille stick for a stamen.

To Make the Tiger Lily

For the petal section, cut a tall peak from a cardboard carton, leaving on four small triangular shapes from the carton's bottom. Make a stamen as described for the tulips.

To Make the Daisies

For each daisy, cut two cups from a plastic-foam carton. Cut the sides of each cup into petals. The stem will be attached to one of the petal sections. The second petal section will be the flower's center.

To Make Basic Flowers

1 Make the petal sections and the flower centers or stamens, following the instructions for the flowers you want to make. Color them with paint or markers.

2 To make a stem, poke two small holes in the bottom of a petal section. Thread a green chenille stick up through one hole, then bend the stick and poke an inch of it down through the second hole. Twist the inch around the stem to secure it. Glue on the flower center or stamen.

3 Arrange your flowers in a vase made from an old bottle that's weighted down with small pebbles and wrapped in gift paper.

More Ideas

Add a little spray of perfume to make scented flowers. Tie a flower to a wrapped present as a special touch. Make a wreath by tying flowers to a piece of painted cardboard cut in an "O" shape. Design a daisy-chain necklace by stringing together lots of egg-carton daisies.

Useful Bulletin Board

You won't get bored with this handy bulletin board.
Create an ever-changing display of photos, notes, and other keepsakes.

You Will Need:

- three plastic-foam egg cartons
- hole punch
- yarn
- pushpins

1 Remove the bottoms from the three cartons. Fasten them together using several pieces of tape placed on the inside.

2 Punch two holes at the top. Tie a piece of yarn through the holes to make a hanger. Use pushpins to mount your items.

More Ideas

Create "thoughts for the day." Write down each thought on a separate piece of paper, and pin a new one to your board each morning.

Use your bulletin board to keep track of homework assignments, or as an art gallery for your drawings.

Frame It!

Egg carton lids make "egg-cellent" frames to display photos of family and friends.

You Will Need:

- cardboard egg carton
- index cards or paper plate
- ruler
- paint
- markers
- construction paper
- ribbon

1 Cut the lid from the egg carton. From the index cards or paper plate, cut circles about 1¾ inch in diameter. Glue the circles to the lid's peaks.

2 Decorate your frame with paint, markers, and construction paper. Add a ribbon hanger. Tape or glue small photos to the white circles.

More Ideas

To make a larger frame, use a lid from a carton that holds two dozen eggs.

Frames filled with pictures of you and your family make special presents for grandparents and aunts and uncles.

Egg-Carton Creatures

These cute critters are fun to play with and to make. Keep several in your room and share some with friends. Everyone's going to want some of these friendly creatures!

You Will Need:

- cardboard egg cartons
- yarn
- toothpick
- one raw egg
- paint
- plastic wiggle eyes
- construction paper
- chenille sticks
- sequins
- plastic-foam egg carton
- markers
- poster board

To Make the Bird on a Nest

Cut a cup from a cardboard egg carton and spread glue around the outside of it. Wrap brown yarn around the cup. With a toothpick, poke a hole in the end of an egg. Carefully enlarge the hole until you're left with about half of the shell. Remove the egg and rinse the shell with water. Glue pieces of yellow yarn inside the nest for straw. Paint the eggshell, and glue it inside the nest. Add wiggle eyes and a paper beak.

To Make the Snail

Cut out two cardboard egg-carton cups and glue them together. Paint the cups. Roll one end of a chenille stick into an oval for the snail's head. Curl the other end of the stick into a flat oval for the bottom of the snail. Glue the chenille-stick body onto the cups. Twist a small piece of chenille stick to the head for antennae. Glue on wiggle eyes.

To Make the Dog

Remove two cups from a cardboard egg carton and trim them so that one has legs and the other has pointy ears. Glue them together as shown. Paint the body. Poke a small hole in the back. With glue, insert a chenille-stick tail. Glue on sequin eyes and a paper nose.

To Make the Octopus

Cut out two cardboard egg-carton cups and glue them together. Paint the cups. Attach eight yarn tentacles with glue. Cut eyes and a mouth from paper, and glue them in place.

To Make the Camel

From a cardboard egg carton, cut a connected two-cup section for the body and a peak for the head. To make the back of the head, trace the bottom of the peak onto a flat piece of lid. Draw on ears and cut out the shape. Paint all these pieces. Poke a hole into the front of the body. With glue, insert a piece of chenille stick for the neck. Glue the other end to the inside of the head. Glue on the back of the head. Attach chenille-stick legs and wiggle eyes with glue.

To Make the Monster

Cut two cups from a plastic-foam egg carton. Cut teeth along the edges of both, and staple or glue the cups together at the back. Color with markers. Glue on poster-board feet and wiggle eyes.

More Ideas

Practically any animal can be made from egg cartons. Look at pictures of animals and think of how to create them using egg cups. You might try a horse, a zebra, a bear, a cat, a bee, a centipede, or a penguin.

Tidy Garden Starter

Make this useful seed starter several weeks before it's warm enough to garden outside. Then give it as a gift to your favorite green thumb.

You Will Need:

- toothpicks
- a dozen eggs
- potting soil
- flower or vegetable seeds
- plastic-foam egg carton
- paper
- markers

1 With a toothpick, poke a hole in one end of each egg. Carefully enlarge the hole and remove the top part of the shell. Remove the eggs and rinse the shells. Poke a small drainage hole in the bottom of each shell. Fill each with potting soil. Plant a seed in each shell.

2 Cut the bottom half from the egg carton, and place the planted shells into the cups. Use flags made from toothpicks and paper to label each shell. Decorate the carton with markers.

3 When the seeds have sprouted and the weather is warm enough, the entire shell with sprout can be planted outdoors.

More Ideas

The bottom of a plastic-foam carton also makes a great bird feeder. Punch a hole at each corner. Tie yarn to each hole, then tie the other ends of the yarn together to make a hanger. Fill the cups with birdseed and hang outside.

Cat Jingle Toy

Cats will have hours of fun batting at this jingly toy.

You Will Need:

- cardboard egg carton
- yarn
- two jingle bells
- masking tape
- tissue paper

1 Cut two cups from the egg carton and trim the tops flat. Poke a hole in the bottom of one cup. Push one end of a piece of yarn through the hole, and tie a knot inside the cup. Place a jingle bell inside the cups and tape them together with masking tape.

2 Cut small squares of tissue paper. Spread a thin layer of glue over the toy, and place the tissue paper pieces onto the glue. Smooth another layer of glue on top of the paper. Slide the second jingle bell onto the yarn and down to the top of the toy. Tie a knot above the bell. Tie a loop at the end of the yarn.

More Ideas

Make a couple of these toys and give them as gifts to friends with cats.

Magnet School

We went fishing for magnets and landed this cool school. They'll "perch" on your refrigerator and keep track of important messages, notes, and pictures.

More Ideas

These fish are so simple to make, you might want to create a school big enough to swim all the way around your fridge.

Add decorations to make your magnets look like specific types of fish, such as catfish, sunfish, or swordfish. Make a magnetic eel by gluing together a chain of cups.

1 Cut out one egg-carton cup for each fish you want to make. Trim each cup to look like the ones in the picture.

2 Color the cups with markers or paint. Cut out fins from crepe paper or tissue paper and glue to the inside top and bottom of each cup.

3 Glue a wiggle eye to one side of each fish. Glue a piece of magnet strip to the opposite side. Use a marker to draw on a mouth.

Finger Puppets and Theater

There are countless ways
To put on great plays.
These puppets are one way we know
To produce a fabulous show!

You Will Need:

- cardboard egg cartons
- paint
- toothpicks
- construction paper
- ribbon
- poster board
- plastic-foam ball
- markers
- plastic-foam egg carton
- yarn
- plastic wiggle eyes
- chopsticks or dowels
- craft sticks
- craft feathers
- foam paper

To Make the Rabbit

Cut one cup from a cardboard egg carton and paint it white. Paint six toothpicks for whiskers. Poke three holes on each side of the cup. Place the whiskers in the holes with glue. Cut eyes, nose, and mouth from construction paper and glue in place. Glue on a ribbon bow. Cut a small strip of poster board. Glue it in a loop to the back of the rabbit's head, leaving enough room so two fingers will fit inside. Your fingers will be the rabbit's ears.

To Make the Rainy-Day Puppet

Cut two peaks from a cardboard egg carton. Cut the top from one peak to make the hat. The taller peak will be the body. Paint the body and hat. Glue a plastic-foam ball to the top of the body. Glue the hat to the plastic-foam ball. Add paper eyes and mouth. Draw on coat buttons and pockets with a marker. To make the umbrella, cut a cup from the plastic-foam egg carton, color it with a marker, and push it onto the end of a toothpick. Poke the other end into the side of the body using a drop of glue.

To Make the Lion

Cut a peak from a cardboard egg carton, trimming it flat around the edges. Glue on feet and ears cut from the carton. Paint the lion's body. Attach a yarn tail and mane with glue. Add wiggle eyes and a paper nose. Draw on a mouth.

To Make the Rooster

Cut a tall peak from a cardboard egg carton, leaving on thin strips for legs. With scissors, trim feet at the bottom of the legs. Paint the rooster. Poke a small hole in the back of rooster near the bottom. Insert a few feathers, using a drop of glue. Glue on a foam-paper comb, beak, and wattle. Add wiggle eyes.

To Make the Theater

Cut the lid from the plastic-foam egg carton. Poke a chopstick or dowel into each side of the lid. Glue on a stage of craft sticks. Add paper curtains and signs.

More Ideas

Write an original play using these puppets as characters, or create your own finger-puppet cast. Hand out invitations to your friends and family. Then, on with the show!

Whirlybird

Go soaring with this nifty helicopter. The propellers turn, but it's up to you to make the chopping noises!

You Will Need:

- plastic-foam egg carton
- ruler
- drinking straw
- metal paper fasteners
- toothpicks
- markers

1 Cut two cups from the egg carton. Glue them together to form the cockpit. Let dry, then carefully cut a small hole (slightly smaller than the width of a drinking straw) in the middle of both the cockpit's roof and floor.

2 From the carton's lid, cut the raised peak, and then cut a small V-shaped notch in the top of it. Make the notch large enough for a drinking straw. Glue it to the top of the cockpit, lining up the two straw holes.

3 Cut two 9½-inch strips from the egg carton lid for propellers. Glue these in an X shape. Let dry, then poke a small hole in the middle of the X. Cut a 3-inch piece of straw. Near one end of the straw, cut two small slits across from one another. Insert a metal paper fastener through the hole in the propellers and into the piece of straw, putting the legs of the metal fastener through the slits you made in the straw and bending them up to secure. Then insert the straw through the holes in the cockpit to put the propellers in place.

4 Cut a 7-inch tailpiece from the side of the egg carton. Cut a slit in the back of the cockpit and insert the tailpiece. For tail propellers, cut two short strips from the lid, glue them in an X shape, and attach with a metal paper fastener.

5 To make landing gear, cut two strips from the side of the carton. Cut a toothpick in half, and poke one half into each strip, using a bit of glue. Place a ¾-inch piece of straw on each toothpick. Using a little glue, stick the ends of the toothpicks into the bottom of the cockpit.

6 Decorate with markers. You may need to glue a small piece of clay in the nose of the helicopter to make it balance.

More Ideas

Tie a piece of fishing line around your helicopter and hang it in your bedroom.

Frosty Ring Toss

"Snow" doubt about it: this game is fun to play by yourself or with friends.

You Will Need:

- cardboard
- construction paper
- poster board
- cardboard egg carton
- paint
- plastic lids from small coffee cans
- glitter
- markers

1 Cut a large circle from the cardboard and cover it with white paper. Cut a hat shape from black paper or poster board. Glue it in place.

2 Cut six cups from the carton and trim their edges nearly flat. Paint five cups black and one cup red. Glue these to the white circle to create a snowman's face. Cut six small circles from white paper. Write a number on each circle, and glue to the cups as shown in the picture.

3 To make the rings, cut the center from the coffee can lids. Cover the rings with glue and sprinkle with glitter to look like snow. To play, set the snowman board on the floor. Stand at a distance, toss the rings, and add up your score.

More Ideas

When playing this game with others, see who can be the first to score 100 points.

"Bee" Mine, Valentine!

Friends and family will love to get this special Valentine's Day card from you.

You Will Need:

- egg carton
- brown yarn
- chenille sticks
- waxed paper
- cardboard
- construction paper
- markers

1 Cut one cup from the egg carton. Cover it with glue. Wind brown yarn around the cup to make it look like a hive.

2 Wrap a yellow chenille stick around your finger or a pencil to make a bee shape. Wrap a black chenille stick around the yellow bee to make stripes. Glue the bee to the hive. Cut wings from waxed paper, and glue them in place. Glue on paper eyes.

3 Cut a large heart from cardboard and cover it with paper. Glue the hive to the center of the heart. Write a Valentine greeting.

More Ideas

Using the hive and bee, make a birthday card with the message, "Have a happy BEE-day!"

WILL YOU MINE, VALENTINE?

Bunches of Baskets

A handmade basket filled with jellybeans or gumdrops makes a wonderful Easter present.

To Make the Bunny Basket

Cut the bottoms from two plastic-foam egg cartons. Cut one in half the long way so you have a row of six cups. Glue this row, upside down, over half of the other carton bottom, leaving the other half open for your basket.

Decorate the row of egg shapes with pompon noses and paper whiskers, eyes, and heart shapes for feet. Make ears from paper and glue one pair to the back of each bunny head. On every other bunny, glue a bow of ribbon. Cut little hats from a cardboard egg carton's peaks. Paint them black and glue each to a circle of black paper. Glue the hats to the remaining bunny heads.

To Make the Two-Cup Basket

Cut a two-cup section from a cardboard egg carton and trim the top edges. Paint the basket. Poke two small holes on opposite sides of the basket. Twist two 8-inch pieces of chenille stick together to form a handle. Push the ends of the handle into the holes, and twist the ends around the rest of the handle to secure.

To Make the One-Cup Mini Baskets

Cut individual cups from a cardboard egg carton and trim the top edges. Paint the cups. Cut 5-inch strips from construction paper and glue to the inside of the cups for handles. Decorate the cups however you'd like. We used sequins and paper cutouts, but glitter and ribbon work well, too.

Isn't there "some-bunny" you know who would like one?

To Make the Four-Cup Basket

Cut a square, four-cup section from a plastic-foam egg carton. Poke two small holes on opposite sides of the basket. Twist two chenille sticks together to form a handle. Attach the handle in the same manner as for the Two-Cup Basket. Make a decoration for the handle by cutting petal shapes into two egg cups. Glue the two cups together, alternating the petals, to make a flower. Poke two holes in the center of the flower. Push a small piece of chenille stick through the holes, and use it to secure the flower to the handle.

More Ideas

Make mini-baskets for any occasion. Fill them with peanuts or candy, and they make great party favors. Decorate some with pictures of your favorite things and use them to hold desk supplies. Paint one in a friend's favorite colors and give it as a jewelry holder.

Four-cup baskets make great "organizer" gifts. Decorate one to match a friend or family member's tastes, then give it as a garden-seed sorter, pocket-change collector, or nail-and-screw caddy.

Collection Display Case

Show off stamps, coins, or other collections in this "see-through" storage container.

You Will Need:

- ruler
- egg carton
- paint
- hole punch
- chenille sticks

1 Mark a ¼-inch border all the way around the top of the egg carton. Carefully cut out the center of the lid, leaving the border. Paint the carton.

2 Use the hole punch to make two holes at each side of the lid. To make the handles, insert the ends of an 8-inch piece of chenille stick into each set of holes. Then twist the ends together to secure.

3 To make the front fastener, punch a hole in the center of the front side of the lid. Punch a corresponding hole on the inside flap. Make a small loop from chenille stick and slide its ends through the holes. Tape the ends to the inside of the carton. Slide another piece of chenille stick through the loop.

More Ideas

Use the display case to wrap a gift. Place a small, wrapped present in the case. It will be two gifts in one.

Paddle Game

Sharpen your hand-to-eye coordination skills with this fun "whack-it-back" game.

You Will Need:

- cardboard egg carton
- craft feathers
- masking tape
- markers
- two small paper plates
- crayons
- paper towel tube

1 To make the shuttlecock, cut out one egg-carton cup and glue feathers around the outside edge. After the glue dries, cover the bottom of the feathers with masking tape. Use markers to color the masking tape and egg cup.

2 To make the paddles, color the two plates with crayons or markers. Cut two 1-inch rings from the tube, and glue one to the back of each plate for handles.

3 To play with a friend, use the paddles to tap the shuttlecock back and forth. To play alone, tap the shuttlecock up in the air with your paddle.

More Ideas

Make four or five paddles and play with a group of friends standing in a circle.

Al Gator

Be a 'gator creator! Make your own Al or Allie Gator. Or create a whole family.

You Will Need:

- cardboard egg cartons
- white paper
- light cardboard
- paint

1 For Al's body, cut the row of peaks from an egg carton, leaving slight extensions at both sides of the second and fourth peaks. Al's legs will be attached to these extensions.

2 To make each of Al's legs, cut out a piece from the bottom of an egg carton. The piece should stretch from the top of one peak over to and including a strip of the side of the carton. Once you've cut four legs in this manner, cut claws into each leg. Fit the top of the peak section of each leg over the extensions you left on in step 1. Glue the legs in place. (Looking at our picture should help you see what we mean.)

3 Cut Al's head from a piece of carton that includes the bottom of two egg cups (these are his eyes) and extends up to include half of the peak in between (this is his nose). Glue his head to the front of his body. Attach white paper teeth with glue.

4 The lower jaw is made from two egg cups: cut one cup in half for the front of the lower jaw; cut out half of one side of the other cup for the back of the lower jaw. Overlap these two pieces, with the bottoms of the two cups facing in opposite directions, and glue together. Add paper teeth. Glue the lower jaw in place beneath the upper jaw.

5 Cut a thin strip of cardboard for a stomach and glue it to the underneath of the body. Cut a tail from the corner of an egg carton lid, and glue it in place. Paint Al.

More Ideas

Wrap bracelets and necklaces around the peaks on Al's back to use him as a jewelry holder. Or place Al on a desk and use his peaks to hold rubber bands.

Masks and More!

Disguise yourself with these masks and costume starters.

To Make the Noses

For each nose, cut a cup from a cardboard egg carton and trim it into the shape shown in the picture. Decorate the nose as described below. To wear it, put a loop of masking tape in the craft nose so it sticks to your nose. (If this doesn't work for you, punch holes in opposite sides of the nose and tie on a string that fits around your head.)

To make the tiger, pig, and Martian noses, paint the cups, then add details with paint or marker. To make the mouse nose, leave the cup gray (or paint a cup gray if it came from a colored carton). Glue on a pink pompon.

To Make the Stick Mask

Cut the lid from a plastic-foam egg carton. Draw a mask design, including eyeholes, onto the lid and cut it out. Color the mask with markers. Outline the edges with glue and sprinkle on glitter. Tape a craft stick to the back of the mask as a handle.

To Make the Tube Mask

Remove the lid from a plastic-foam egg carton. Hold it to your face and place two fingers where your eyes are. Remove it from your face, leaving your fingers there. Draw eyeholes, then cut them out. Decorate the lid with construction paper cutouts. Cover a paper towel tube with paper and add cut-paper decorations. Glue it to the back of the mask for a handle.

Use one by itself, or create a costume to go with it. Your friends will wonder, "Who is that masked kid?"

To Make the Groovy Glasses

To make the frames, cut a two-cup section from a plastic-foam egg carton. Cut the bottoms from the cups to make eyeholes. Color a piece of plastic wrap with a marker and cut out two circles for lenses. Glue the lenses to the inside of the frames. Color the frames with a marker. Poke holes at opposite sides of the frames. Insert the end of a chenille stick into each hole and twist it around the frame to secure. Try your glasses on, bending the chenille sticks over your ears. Trim the sticks to fit your head.

More Ideas

Throw a "mask"-erade party where you and your guests each make a costume starter. Or give noses out as party favors and have your guests design costumes to go with them.

Make an elephant's trunk by gluing a stack of gray egg cups together. Poke holes in the sides of the bottom cup on the stack. Tie on a string to wear it around your head.

No-Snow Snowman

Here's a snowman you can build without getting your hands cold. And this wintry friend will stick around even when the temperature soars.

You Will Need:

- plastic-foam egg carton
- twig
- white paper towels or napkins
- poster board
- buttons
- construction paper or foam paper
- marker
- fabric scrap

1 Cut two rows of three cups from a white egg carton. (If you use a color other than white, you'll need to add extra layers of ripped paper in step 2.) Place a thin twig in between the two pieces, between the first and second cups. Tape the cups together to form the body, making sure the twig "arms" are secure.

2 In a small bowl, combine equal amounts of glue and water. Tear small pieces of the paper towels or napkins and dip them into the glue mixture. Use these pieces to cover the entire surface of the snowman. Cut a 4-inch square from the poster board and cover it in the same manner. Let the snowman and the square base dry.

3 Glue the snowman to the square base. Decorate him with buttons, paper eyes, and marker. Tie a small strip of fabric around his neck for a scarf.

More Ideas

Create other figures in this way. Make a clown by covering the body with pieces of multicolored tissue paper and decorating it with pompon buttons, a red nose, and yarn hair.

Make an ant by laying the body on its side and covering it with black tissue paper pieces. Add chenille-stick legs and antennae, and paper eyes.

3-D Apple

This apple decoration makes an "egg-stra" nice gift for a teacher.

You Will Need:

- plastic-foam egg carton
- paint or markers
- string or ribbon

1 On the lid of a plastic-foam egg carton, draw two apples of the same size. Draw a stem on only one apple. Cut out the apple shapes.

2 Cut a slit in each shape in the following manner: The shape with the stem should be slit from the bottom to the center of the apple. Slit the other piece from the top down to the center. Fit the apple together by sliding the slits into one another. Spread some glue around the slits.

3 Color the apple with paint or markers. Poke a hole in the stem, and attach a loop of string or ribbon for a hanger.

More Ideas

All kinds of fruit can be made in this manner. Create enough 3-D fruit to fill an entire fruit bowl and use it as a centerpiece. Or make 3-D fruits and vegetables to use as part of a Thanksgiving cornucopia decoration.

Sunflower Magnet

Add some sunshine to your family's day with this cheerful magnet.

You Will Need:

- egg carton
- marker
- glitter
- cardboard
- felt or construction paper
- sunflower seeds
- magnet strips

1 Cut two cups from an egg carton and trim their sides to look like petals. Use a marker to color your flowers. Trace around each flower petal with glue and sprinkle with gold glitter.

2 Cut out a cardboard circle larger than the bottom of an egg cup. Cut out leaves from felt or paper and glue them to the circle. Glue one flower section to the center of the leaves. Then glue the second flower section inside the first, alternating flower petals.

3 Cover the flower center with glue, then set sunflower seeds into the glue. Attach magnet strips to the back.

More Ideas

Make a garden of flower magnets. Try some of the flower patterns on page 18 or design your own colorful flowers.

Deck the Halls

Make your Christmas season merry and bright with these festive decorations.

You Will Need:

- cardboard egg cartons
- ribbon
- paint
- glitter
- lightweight cardboard
- ruler
- buttons
- chenille sticks
- jingle bells
- wooden and plastic beads
- plastic-foam egg carton

To Make the Glittery Ornaments

For each ornament, cut two cups from a cardboard egg carton. For round ornaments, trim each cup's edges flat. Tie a piece of ribbon into a loop, place the knot inside the cups, and glue the cups together. For the arched ornament, trim the two cups as in the picture. Poke a hole in the bottom of one cup, insert a loop of ribbon, and tape its ends to the inside of the cup. Glue the two cups together by their tips. Decorate your ornaments with paint and glitter.

To Make the Candy Cane

Cut 20 cups from cardboard egg cartons. Paint ten white and ten red. Measure across the bottom of one cup. Cut nineteen circles from cardboard that are about ¼-inch wider than the cup's bottom. These are spacers to hold the cups apart. Poke a hole in the bottom of each cup and in the center of each circle. Twist a button onto the end of a chenille stick. Thread on a white cup, spacer, red cup, spacer, white cup, and so on until only the last ¾-inch of chenille stick is showing. Twist a jingle bell onto the end. Gently bend into a cane shape. Add a ribbon hanger.

You'll find ornaments to spruce up a tree, and bells to jingle on a door. Once you start crafting them, you'll want to make more and more.

To Make the Angel Ornaments

For each angel, paint a face and hair onto a wooden bead. Fold a 7-inch piece of chenille stick in half. Thread the wooden bead onto the chenille stick, forming the fold of the stick into a small "halo" above the head. Thread a two-hole button on beneath the head, then tie on a piece of ribbon. Cut a cup from a white plastic-foam carton for the skirt. Poke a hole in the top of the cup, and thread it on next. Thread on a small bead and push it tightly against the skirt. Spread the ends of the chenille stick apart. Thread a bead onto each end, and bend the ends up to keep the beads from sliding off. Tie a ribbon hanger to the top.

To Make the Silver Bells

For the bells, cut peaks from a cardboard egg carton and trim the edges. Cover them inside and out with silver paint. Sprinkle them with glitter and let dry. Tie a piece of ribbon to a jingle bell and make a knot about an inch above the bell. Poke a small hole in the top of an egg-carton bell, and pull the ribbon through the hole until the knot is against the inside of the bell. Tie a knot in the ribbon on top of the bell. Repeat this for each silver bell. Gather all the ribbons together, and tie a knot for a hanger.

More Ideas

Make a long chain to wrap around the tree by threading individual painted egg cups onto a piece of string. Add glitter or other decorative touches.

Create a wreath by threading a chain of cups onto a string and tying the two ends of the string together to form a circle. Add a bow, and glue on small pinecones.

Compact Binoculars

Enjoy the sights with your own pair of binoculars.

You Will Need:
- plastic-foam egg carton
- yarn
- hole punch
- construction paper
- marker
- paint
- toothpaste cap

1 Cut the end from an egg carton, so that you have a two-cup piece and the lid above it. Glue the lid portion and the cup portion shut. Glue a piece of yarn around the seam.

2 Cut eyeholes from the bottom of the two egg cups. In the lid directly opposite these holes, cut holes of the same size. With the hole punch, make a hole on each side of the binoculars. Tie a piece of yarn to the holes to make a strap.

3 Glue on a piece of black paper to cover the bottom of the binoculars. Color the binoculars with a marker. Add details cut from paper. Glue a painted toothpaste cap to the top.

More Ideas
Instead of the yarn strap, glue a craft stick to one side to make opera glasses.

Egg-Carton Carryall

Transport pencils, notepads, and much more in this super shoulder bag.

You Will Need:
- plastic-foam egg carton
- hole punch
- ribbon
- felt
- ruler

1 Cut the lid of the egg carton in half. Glue the two halves together at their edges to form the purse. To make the shoulder strap, punch a hole on each side of the bag near the top. Tie a piece of ribbon to these holes.

2 Cut a piece of felt big enough to cover the purse. Spread glue all over the purse. Wrap the felt around it as you would gift wrap, gluing the folds of felt in place.

3 Cut a 7-inch strip of felt for the bag's latch. Glue the bottom of the latch onto the back of the bag. Cut a small strip of felt that is about 1 1/2 inches longer than the latch is wide. Glue both ends of this strip to the front of the bag as a fastener in which to tuck the latch.

More Ideas
Make a longer shoulder bag by cutting only a short end off of each of two lids, and gluing them together. Or make a mini-bag by using two small sections from one lid.

Carton Crawlers

These caterpillars won't turn into butterflies, but they will turn any space into a more pleasant one.

You Will Need:

- cardboard egg cartons
- paint
- chenille stick
- plastic wiggle eyes
- yarn
- construction paper

To Make the Straight Caterpillar

Cut a row of six cups from an egg carton to make the body of the caterpillar. To make legs, cut a small section from both sides of each cup. Paint the caterpillar and let it dry. To make antennae, poke two small holes in the top of the caterpillar's head. Poke a piece of chenille stick into each hole, using glue. Curl the ends of the antennae. Glue on wiggle eyes.

To Make the Wiggly Caterpillar

Cut the twelve cups from an egg carton. Paint each cup inside and out. Poke a small hole in the bottom of each cup. Tie a knot at one end of a piece of yarn— this will be the caterpillar's nose. String the other end of the yarn through the holes in the cups. When the twelve cups are strung together, knot the other end. Add eyes cut from construction paper.

More Ideas

Make caterpillars of all sizes. String together cups from two or three egg cartons to make a super-long wiggly caterpillar. Or cut a three-cup section to make a small straight caterpillar.

Cut out a giant construction-paper leaf for your caterpillars to "nibble" on.

Perfect Party Favors

Make your guests feel special with handmade party favors and place cards.

You Will Need:

- cardboard egg cartons
- paint
- sequins
- construction paper
- yarn
- ruler
- aluminum foil
- chenille sticks
- thin ribbon
- plastic wiggle eyes
- toothpick
- markers
- thin cardboard
- glitter

To Make the Rabbit and Cat Trinket Cups

For each trinket cup, cut one egg cup from a carton and trim it into the shape in the picture. Paint the cup. Add details with sequins, paper, yarn, and paint. Fill with small candies.

To Make the Mini Treasure Box

Cut two cups from an egg carton and trim the edges flat. Paint the outsides of the cups. Press a 3-inch square of aluminum foil into each cup. Trim the excess. Glue a piece of chenille stick or other trim to the edge of each cup. Lay a 14-inch piece of ribbon on a flat surface. Spread glue on the middle 4 inches of the ribbon, leaving 5 unglued inches on each end. Put one cup on top of the other, and place them at one end of the glued section of ribbon. Wrap the long end of the ribbon up and over the top of the box. Tie to close.

To Make the Flower Nut Cup

Cut one cup from an egg carton. Scallop the edges with scissors, and paint the cup. For a base, draw and cut out a section of leaves from paper. Then cut a flower with long petals. Glue the leaf section and the flower together. Glue the cup to the middle of the flower. Fill with peanuts.

Or use some to turn a family meal into a festive occasion.

To Make the Spider Place Card

Cut one cup from an egg carton and paint it black. Poke four evenly spaced holes on each side of the cup. Insert a chenille stick into each hole, using a bit of glue. Bend each stick into a leg shape. Glue a black paper circle to the bottom of the cup. Add wiggle eyes. Make a sign by folding a piece of paper over a toothpick and gluing shut. Write your guest's name on the sign. Glue the toothpick in place on one of the spider's front legs.

To Make the Graduation-Cap Place Card

Cut one cup from an egg carton. Cut a square from a piece of cardboard. Paint both pieces black and glue the square to the bottom of the cup to form a cap. Glue a piece of yarn to the middle of the cap's top, and tie and fringe its end to form a tassel. Cover the glued end of yarn with a small square of black paper. Write a message with a silver marker. Use as a place card, or turn it over to fill with nuts or candy.

To Make the Hanukkah Place Card

Cut one cup from an egg carton, leaving on the side "legs" as shown. Paint it blue. From a piece of cardboard, cut a Star of David. Trace the star onto blue paper and cut it out. Glue the two stars together. Decorate the star with glitter, and write a guest's name. Cut a small slit in the top of the cup and insert a point of the star. Make one for each guest.

More Ideas

There's no end to the party favors you can create from egg cartons. Most round objects can be made from egg cups. For example, make soccer ball, basketball, and hockey puck favors for a sports-themed party. Or throw a summer party, and make small egg-cup suns with construction-paper rays.

Fourth of July Wreath

Reach for the stars with this patriotic Independence Day wreath.

You Will Need:

- plastic-foam egg carton
- tissue paper
- foil stars or construction paper
- ribbon
- yarn

1 Remove the lid from the egg carton and discard. Cut the cup section of the carton in half the long way, so you have two six-cup rows.

2 Staple the two six-cup sections together, end to end, with the open part of the cups facing out. This will make a circle. Add some glue or staples between each cup to help hold them together.

3 Crumple a piece of tissue paper into a ball, and glue the ball into an egg cup. Fill each of the twelve cups in this manner.

4 Decorate the outside of the cups with foil stars or stars cut from construction paper. Glue a ribbon to the bottom of the wreath. Tie a yarn hanger to the top, and hang on a door or wall.

More Ideas

Design egg-carton wreaths for other occasions. Welcome the first day of autumn with a wreath made with yellow, red, and orange tissue paper, and decorated with cutouts of fall leaves. Make a get-well wreath to cheer up a friend who is under the weather. Use brightly colored tissue paper and glue on flowers and suns from construction paper. Or try making a Superbowl wreath using tissue paper of your favorite team's colors, and cutouts of footballs and helmets.

Turtle Paperweight

This trusty turtle will hold down the loose papers on your desk.

You Will Need:

- egg carton
- small pebbles
- small piece of cardboard
- craft sticks
- paint
- marker

1 Cut one cup from an egg carton to make the turtle's shell. Fill the cup with small pebbles. Glue a piece of cardboard to the bottom of the cup. When the glue is dry, trim the edges to match the turtle's shape.

2 Cut a head, a pointy tail, and legs from craft sticks. Glue them in place on the bottom of the turtle. Paint the turtle. Draw on eyes with a marker.

More Ideas

Keep your paperweight on the kitchen counter to hold down recipe cards, or place it near a phone to keep track of messages.

Thread Caddy

Here's a great gift for anyone you know who likes to sew.

You Will Need:

- egg carton
- markers
- felt
- toothpick or knitting needle
- small spools of thread

1 Decorate the lid of a clean egg carton with markers and scraps of felt. (We used an eighteen-count egg carton, but a carton for a dozen eggs will work well, too.) With a toothpick or knitting needle, poke a hole in the lid over each of the egg cups.

2 Place a small spool of thread into each of the cups, then poke the ends of the thread up through the holes. You may need to use a sewing needle to guide the ends of the thread through the holes.

3 Close the lid, and pull up pieces of thread as you need them.

More Ideas

An egg carton also makes a perfect button box. Decorate the outside of a clean carton with markers and old buttons, and use the compartments inside to store buttons.

Game Time!

Egg cartons can be the starting point for all sorts of games. Here are four of our favorites. If you're game, try inventing some of your own. Have fun, and let the games begin!

You Will Need:

- cardboard egg cartons
- paint
- construction paper
- markers
- plastic-foam egg cartons
- marbles
- twelve buttons of four different colors
- a die
- various items for decoration: chenille sticks, plastic wiggle eyes, waxed paper, and toothpicks

To Make the Memory-Match Game

Cut the twelve cups from a cardboard egg carton and paint them. Cut out twelve 1-inch circles from paper. Draw a picture on each one, making six pairs of pictures that are the same (for example, draw two kites, two stars, and so on). Glue one picture into each cup.

To play, place all the cups face-down. Each player turns over two cups and looks at the pictures. If they match, the player keeps the pair. If not, the cups are returned to the face-down position. It is then the next player's turn. The game continues until all the cups are matched up. The player with the most pairs wins. For a more challenging game, add another twelve cups.

To Make the Marble-Pitch Game

Decorate the lid of an egg carton with construction paper. Remove the front flap from the carton. Cut twelve circles from paper and number them 1 to 12. Glue these, in random order, inside the cups of the carton. To play the game, set the open carton on the floor with the lid propped against the wall or another solid surface. Place a piece of tape on the floor at least 5 feet from the carton. Each player gets six marbles. Players take turns standing behind the tape and pitching the marbles toward the cups. To score, add up the numbers in the cups where marbles landed. The first player with 100 points wins.

To Make the Beehive Game

Cut a row of six cups from a cardboard egg carton. Paint them yellow to look like a beehive. We decorated our hive with the bee described on page 27. To play, place the hive on the floor against a wall. Place a piece of tape about 3 feet from the hive. Each player gets five marbles, which represent bees. Players take turns sitting behind the tape and rolling marbles one at a time toward the six openings of the hive. Each time a marble remains in a hive, the player gets one point. The first to reach 20 points wins.

Treat Tree

This sweet tree is two crafts in one—it's a colorful Christmas decoration and a handy candy holder.

You Will Need:

- three cardboard egg cartons
- ruler
- paint
- 14- inch-by-17-inch piece of cardboard
- Christmas gift wrap
- heavy white paper
- chenille sticks
- small box (from crackers or cookies)
- aluminum foil
- ribbon or yarn

1 Cut the bottoms from three egg cartons and lay them side by side. With a ruler, draw a triangular tree shape extending from the top middle of the uppermost of the three cartons, down to the bottom of the third carton. (Looking at our picture should help you see what we mean.) Cut out the tree shape and glue the pieces together. Paint the tree green.

2 Wrap the piece of cardboard with gift wrap, taping the folded edges of the gift wrap to the back. From white paper, cut a triangle that's slightly larger than the tree. Glue it to the wrapped cardboard, leaving room for a trunk.

3 Shape chenille sticks to the tree and tape their ends at the back of the tree. Glue the tree onto the white triangle you made in step 2.

4 Cut off the bottom section of the small box and trim it into a tree-trunk shape, leaving the bottom of the box intact. Paint it brown. Fit it to the bottom of the tree and glue in place.

5 Crumple a small square of aluminum foil. Unfold it and cut out a star shape. Glue the star to the top of the tree. Poke a hole at either side of the tree top. Tie a loop of ribbon or yarn through the holes to make a wall hanger.

6 Hang up your tree and fill its trunk with candy.

More Ideas

To make your tree even more festive, glue glitter to the end of each branch.

Make a forest of trees, decorating each one differently. Fill each tree with a different kind of goody.

Title Index

Subject Index